Written by Sue Graves
Illustrated by Daniel Haworth (Advocate)
Designed by Blue Sunflower Creative

Language consultant: Betty Root

This is a Parragon Publishing book
This edition published in 2003

Parragon Publishing
Queen Street House
4 Queen Street
Bath, BA1 1HE, UK

ISBN 1-40542-699-3
Printed in China

Sam Duckling Swims

p

Notes for Parents

Reading with your child is an enjoyable and rewarding experience. These **Gold Stars** reading books encourage and support children who are learning to read.

The **Gold Stars** reading books are filled with fun stories, familiar vocabulary, and amusing pictures. Sharing these books with your child will ensure that reading is fun. It is important, at this early stage, for children to enjoy reading and succeed. Success creates confidence.

Starting to read

Start by reading the book aloud to your child, taking time to talk about the pictures. This will help your child to see that pictures often give clues about the story.

Over a period of time, try to read the same book several times so that your child becomes familiar with the story and the words and phrases. Gradually your child will want to read the book aloud with you. It helps to run your finger under the words as you say them.

Occasionally, stop and encourage your child to continue reading aloud without you. Join in again when your child needs help. This is the next step toward helping your child become an independent reader.

Finally, your child will be ready to read alone. Listen carefully to your child and give plenty of praise. Remember to make reading an enjoyable experience.

Using your Gold Stars stickers

Remember to use the **Gold Stars** stickers at the back of the book as a reward for effort as well as achievement. Learning to read is an exciting challenge for every child.

Remember these four important stages:

- Read the story **to** your child.
- Read the story **with** your child.
- Encourage your child to read **to you**.
- Listen to your child read **alone**.

This is Sam Duckling.
Sam lives by the pond.

He lives with Mommy Duck
and the other ducklings.

"Jump in and swim," said Mommy Duck one day.

The ducklings jumped in the pond.

Splash!

Splash!

Splash! They swam and swam.

But Sam didn't jump in.

"Jump in and swim," said Mommy Duck. "It's fun!"

Sam looked into the water.

"The water is too deep," he said. "I'll stay here."

"Jump in and swim," said Mommy Duck. "It's fun!"

Sam put his wing in the water.

"The water is too cold," said
Sam. "I'll stay here."

"Quack, quack!" said the ducklings. "Swim with us, Mommy! Swim with us!"

Mommy Duck went off with the ducklings. Sam began to cry.

Just then, Frog popped up.
He popped up out of the water.

"Hello, Sam," said Frog.
"Come and swim. It's fun!"

"I don't want to," said Sam.
"The water is too deep and
too cold."

Frog sat by Sam.

"I'll help you swim," he said.

Frog got a lily pad.

"Sit on the lily pad, Sam," he said.

Sam sat on the lily pad.

Frog pulled Sam along.

"Now, splash your feet," said Frog.

Sam splashed his feet.

"Quack, quack!" said Sam.
"This is fun!"

"Now get off the lily pad," said Frog.

Sam got off the lily pad.

"I'm swimming!" said Sam.

"Quack, quack!" said Mommy Duck. "Well done, Sam!"

Quack, quack!

Read these words. Look back
in the book and find the words.

Sam

Mommy
Duck

pond

ducklings

Frog

lily pad

Gold Stars reading books are for
children who are beginning
to read.

- Familiar, repeated vocabulary
- Short sentences
- Large, clear type
- Pictures that support the text
- Review activity